All Ki[illegible]
Writing

Book 2

Contents

1	Writing directions	2
2	Presenting an argument	9
3	Writing poetry	16
4	Writing to persuade	24
5	Reporting	32
6	Taking notes	41
7	Justifying	47
8	Reflecting	54
	Writing chart	63
	Note to the teacher	64

Cambridge University Press
Cambridge London New York New Rochelle Melbourne Sydney

When we write directions we have to take great care or people will get lost or confused. This unit helps you to write directions properly.

Look carefully at this street map.

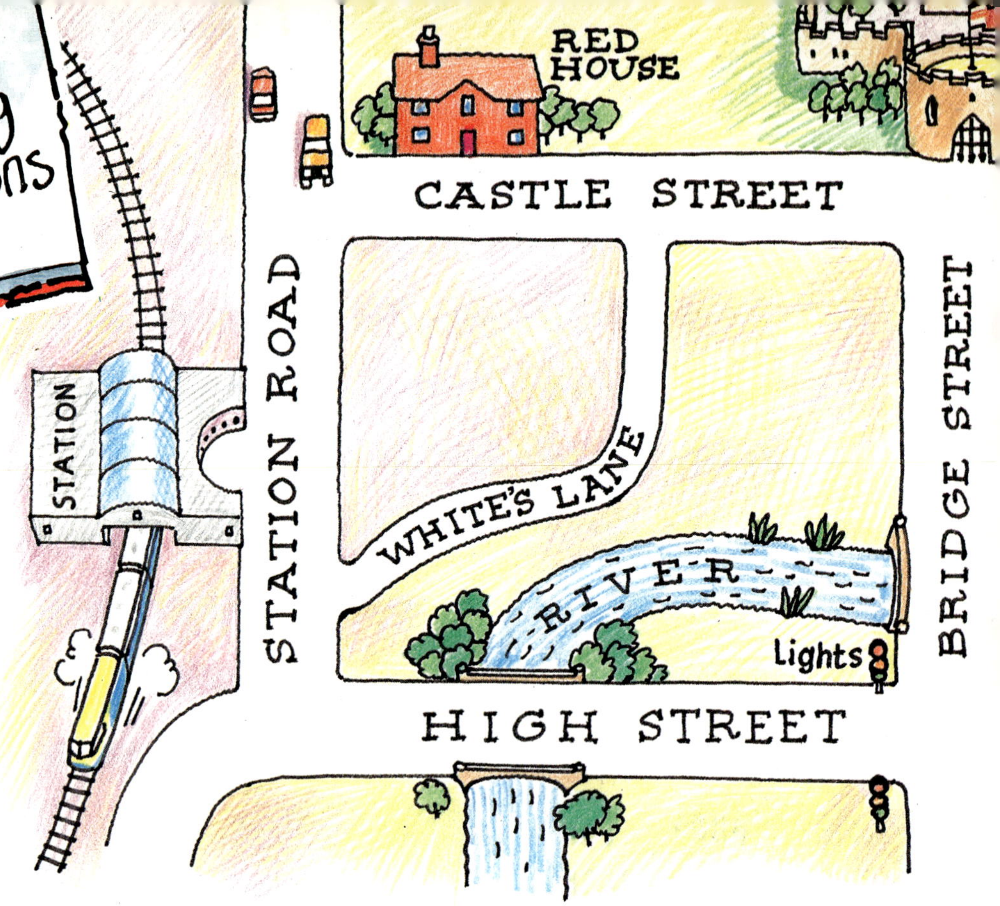

If you were writing directions for someone to go from the Red House to the school you might write them like this:

> When leaving the house turn left along Castle Street.
> Take the second turning on the right into Bridge Street opposite Castle Gate.
> Go along Bridge Street over the bridge.
> When you come to the traffic lights turn left along the High Street.
> Take the third turning left into Gordon Street.
> Take the first turning right into Mount Road.
> The school is a short distance along Mount Road on your left.

What you do

1 Write the same sort of directions as those above to take someone from the school to the Red House.

2 You meet a visitor in the car park. She wants to go boating. How would you direct her to the boat house?

3 You meet a visitor by the castle who is in a hurry to catch a train. Tell him the quickest way to the railway station.

4 Where am I if I can hear children, see an ancient building on my right, and am likely to get wet if I slip?

Giving exact directions is not easy.
Writing them down for someone can be even more difficult.

When giving someone directions in writing to find a place in a town we need to remember

- **a** to use street names;
- **b** state the number of turnings;
- **c** use landmarks like the castle and the bridge to help;
- **d** start a new line for each new direction.

What you do

1. Write out directions for someone who is a stranger to your town telling them how to get from your house to your school.
2. Aunt Polly is coming to visit you. She has never been to your town before. Write directions for her to get from the edge of the town to your house.

Note
You may live in the country and come to school by bus. If so, ask your teacher to suggest a suitable journey for you to write about.

Desert journey

Sometimes there are no street names and few landmarks. Travellers have to use a compass.

Before you go any further make sure you know how to read a compass. Talk about this with your teacher if you are not sure.

What you do

You are going to cross the desert from Omar to the Ancient Ruins of Ghezz. Write out your directions for the journey starting like this:

Go north-east (NE) from Omar to the Geer Oasis.
Camp for the night and then go north (N) to the . . .

Complete your directions for the journey.

There is a pass through the Stony Mountains which can be seen from the Jamil village, but it is sometimes blocked by falling boulders and raided by bandits. Beware of the Taureg camp; they do not welcome strangers and can be hostile. You may wish to go north of the mountains. It will be further but safer. The choice is yours.

Desert diary

The desert journey you have just plotted took place in 1895. It took 12 days and they faced many dangers . . .

. . . sand storms

. . . and bandits

There were two men and one woman on the journey. They were called Richard Pope, Harry King and Joyce Trump. Richard kept a diary.

This is the first page.

What you do

Complete Richard's diary for the desert crossing from October 1st to October 12th.

You can imagine all sorts of dangers from sand storms, bandits, getting lost, accidents to your companions, losing water bottles and so on.

Make it as exciting as you can. If you don't feel able to write the whole diary, plan it with a friend and then write some pages each.

Rescue

The good ship SS Speedwell has hit a rock and is sinking. It is in position **F** on the map. Over in position **A** is the lifeboat of which you are in charge. The map shows the course the lifeboat will have to steer to reach the sinking ship and take the crew to Kingstown.

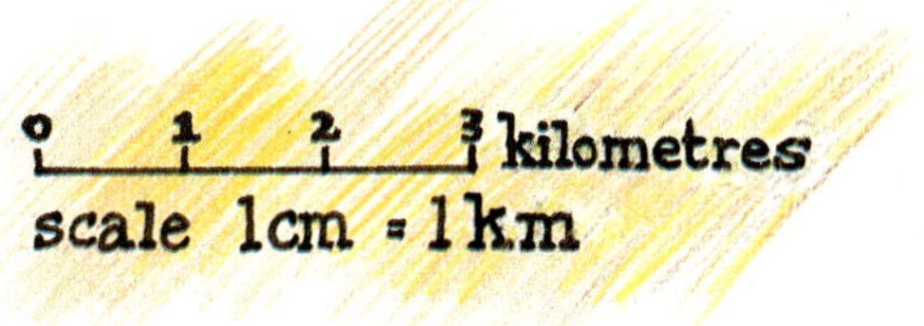

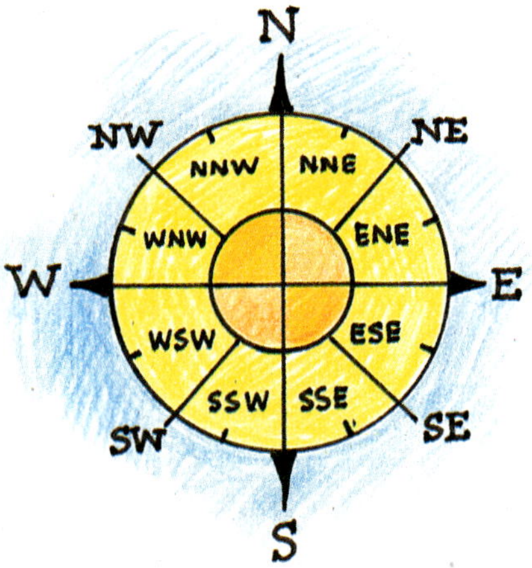

What you do

As coxswain – the person in charge – of the lifeboat you have to write down the course directions for your crew.

For each part of the voyage you have to write directions and distances plus any sightings which may help the helmsman and look-outs.

It is night, so you have to navigate the narrow channels with care.

The first part of the passage is done for you:

> A to B steer NE for 1½ kms . You will see Larn light to the south. B to C. Steer for 4 kms To the west you will see the . . .

Now you finish the directions.

Secret agent

Do you know these signs and symbols?
They are used on maps. Learn them before you try the exercise below.

Church with tower

Lighthouse

Windmill

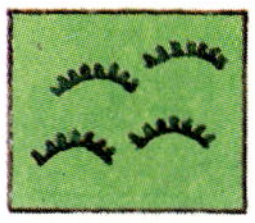
Marsh

Castle

Wood

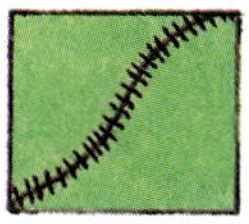
Railway

Marie was a secret agent. She had spent the last month in enemy country gathering vital information on their troops and new weapons.

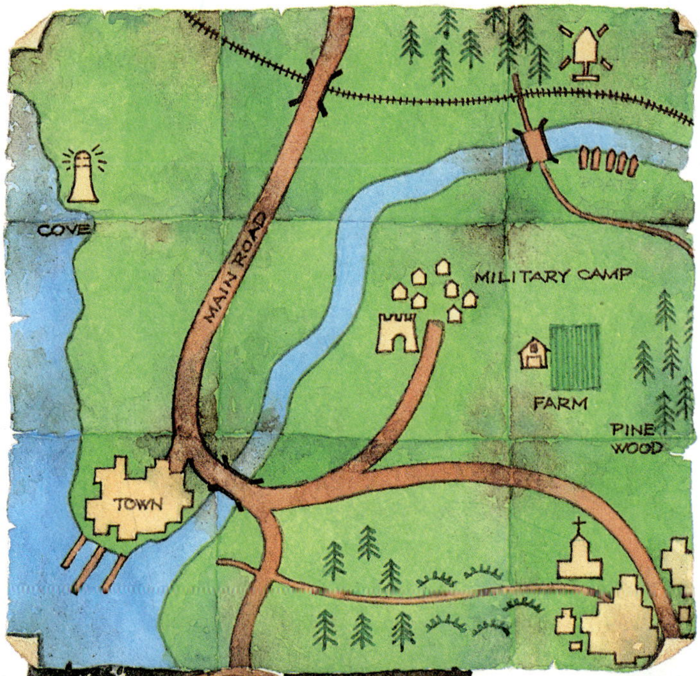

She was on her way back to Britain and had hidden all night in the church tower of a small village only three miles from the coast. She was cramped and cold, but she knew she must remain there until dawn if she was to avoid the enemy troops.

As the sun rose she stood and looked carefully over the parapet of the tower.

Below her she could see the lights of the village. Far to the north she could see a windmill standing on a ridge with a large dense wood lying to the west of it. In the distance to the north-west she suddenly caught the flash of a lighthouse, growing dimmer as the sun strengthened. Her heart beat faster. This must be the light Jacques had spoken of. Below it would lie the hidden cove with safety in the form of a fast launch. But how was she to reach it?

She turned slowly, looking carefully at the countryside around her . . .

What you do

1 Using the map, describe what Marie saw as she looked around from the tower.

2 Plot a route for her to take to get her safely to the cove and the boat. Remember bridges and roads will be watched by soldiers. Stay as hidden as you can in woods. How will you cross the river?

3 When you have plotted Marie's course, step-by-step as if giving her instructions, write out her escape as an exciting story.

Treasure island

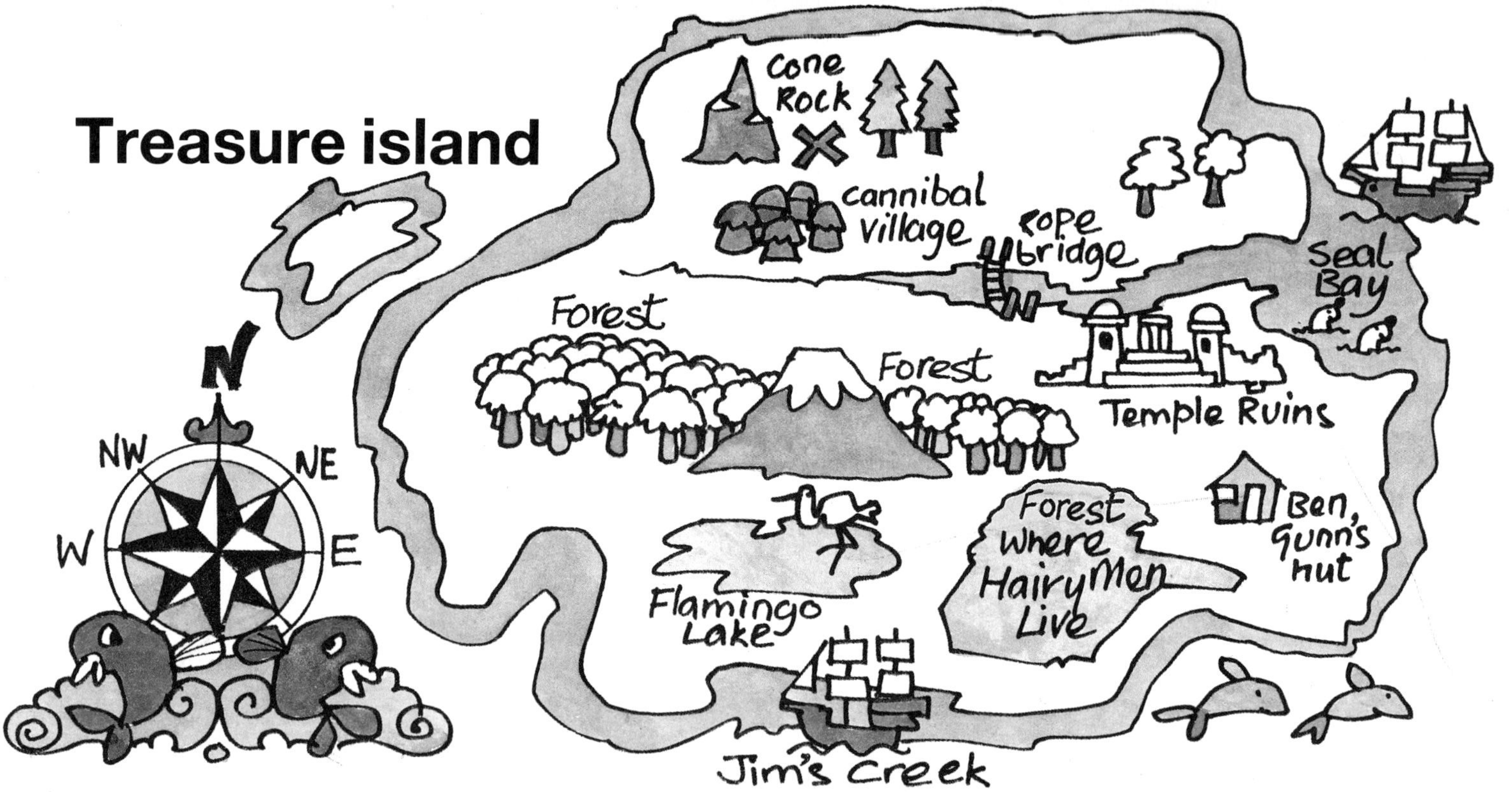

Captain Flint left buried treasure on this island. When the island was discovered an old chest was found and in it an old map and instructions. Many of the words were missing.

From Jim's Creek go ..... to Fla......
L........ Then go .... until you
reach B...................... t. Take
care as you pass the Forest where
the H.............. live. Go N.W. to ......
.... Some people say these
ruins are haunted. A short distance away is the
.... b......... over the river. Be very quiet,
just to the .... is the .... If
they hear you you are done for. East you see
S........ B..... Look inland for the tall P.........
Beyond that you will see .... Half way
between the two you see
my marker. Flint

What you do

1 Study Flint's map and message carefully. Rewrite the whole of the message putting in the missing words.

2 Imagine you are the person who found the map and message. Tell the story of your landing on the island and your journey to seek the treasure. You are certain to have plenty of adventures. Good luck.

Unit 2 Presenting an argument

Have you a favourite place where you and your friends like to meet . . .

Like this . . .

. . . or this

It may be a park, an adventure playground, someone's backyard or even under a lamp-post. It is the place where you meet to decide what to do, where to go or what to play. Most boys and girls have a favourite place for meeting and playing.

Or perhaps this . . .

What you do

1 Discussion time
Have a class discussion and hear where your classmates meet. Perhaps your teacher can remember his or her favourite play place. You may know where your Mum or Dad used to meet their friends; if not, ask them.

2 Write a little about your meeting place. Say why you think it's a good place to meet. (If you haven't got a special place, think of one you would like to have and describe it.) What sort of things do you do there? What games do you play?

3 Suppose one day someone came along and said that you couldn't use your special place any more.
Perhaps the park is going to close or the playground shut. How would you feel? What could you do to try and stop the park or playground being closed? Write about it.

Were you able to put forward a good argument to save your special playground?
This unit helps you to learn how to present a good argument.

Troubles at Rushington Green

Rushington is part of a large city. There isn't much open space left except a place everyone calls The Green. Years ago Rushington was a village outside the town and this was the village green.

The people of Rushington like their green. It has grass, trees and even a stream. Older people walk their dogs there, joggers jog there, teenagers play football there and children of all ages play there most of the time.

Then one day an article appeared in the *Rushington Echo.*

FACTORY TO BE BUILT AT RUSHINGTON

Yesterday Eston City Council gave planning permission for a factory to be built on Rushington Green. The factory will be built for R G Sykes & Co. who make electrical and engineering products. The council stated that Rushington Green was only waste land, not a proper park and would make an ideal place for a factory.

When Rushington people saw the article they were very angry. Can you imagine what the local people said?
People, even the children, talked about nothing else.

The people of Rushington decided to fight to save their green. They held a public meeting and decided to write at once to Mr Brown, the Clerk to the City Council, objecting to the factory.

They had to remember four things when they wrote their letter:

1 To make their letter short and to the point. It will be read by busy people.
2 To give reasons for not wanting the factory. It would be no use just writing to say that they didn't want it.
3 To argue for all the residents – the old, young and sick – not for selfish or personal reasons.
4 To keep calm. It wouldn't help to write a letter like this:

> Brown,
> Keep your factory off our green or else watch out.
> signed Angry Rushingtonian.

What you do

1 Imagine you are the people of Rushington at the public meeting. Discuss all the reasons you want to put forward against the factory.

2 Write your letter to Mr Brown. Remember to make a good case, you have to give facts and reasons, stay calm, keep your letter to the point.
Argue for everyone, not just for yourself. It is much better to say the noise will keep everyone awake rather than 'the noise will keep me awake'. But your concern must be genuine.

Discussion time

3 When you have finished your letter, get into groups of four. Read your letters to each other. Choose the best one.
Now listen to the best letters from the other groups. Choose the letter to send to Mr Brown. It is important for everyone to know why that letter was chosen and why it made the best case against the factory.

Another point of view

Not everyone is against the factory.

Tom Stone the builder hasn't put up a new house for years. He has some empty old houses he would like to pull down and replace with new ones, but no-one is moving into the area.

Bill Smith is a teenager who lives in Rushington. He left school a year ago but he hasn't found a job yet.

Jim Smale worked for a small firm that had to shut down. He is out of work as well.

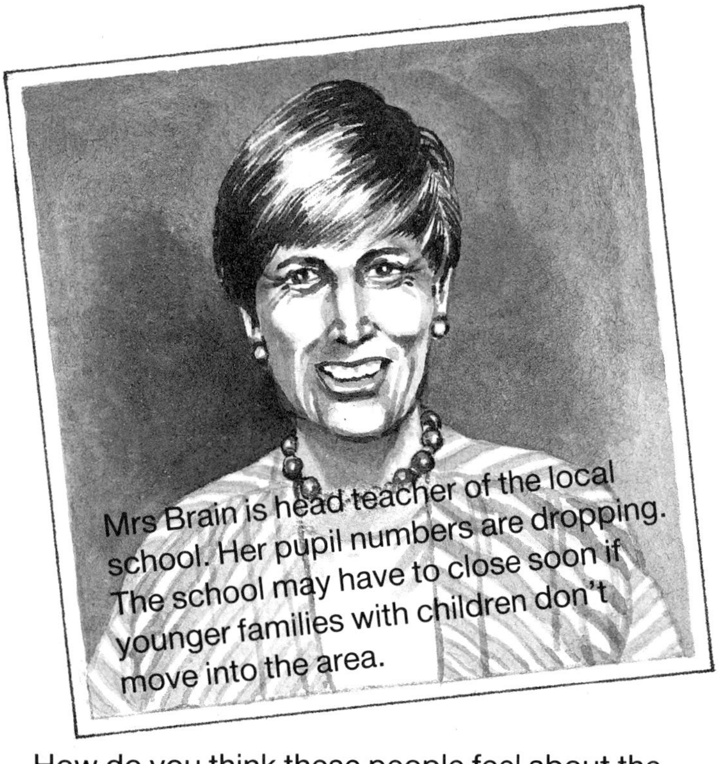

Mrs Brain is head teacher of the local school. Her pupil numbers are dropping. The school may have to close soon if younger families with children don't move into the area.

Mrs Green owns the local shop. She sells groceries. Business isn't very good. Local people haven't much money to spend and they go to the cheaper supermarkets in the city centre.

How do you think these people feel about the new factory?

Mrs Green, Mrs Brain, Bill, Jim and Tom Stone wanted the factory built very much.
They argued against the other Rushington folk and they felt they had a good case.

What you do

Discussion time

1 Hold a discussion about the feelings of the people above. Why do they each want the factory? They all have different but important reasons. Some of the class can play the parts of Bill, Jim and the rest and speak for them.
Make a list of all the reasons for wanting the factory in Rushington.

2 On your own, write down any other people who may be glad to see the factory. Write a sentence or so beside their name to say why they want it.

3 Write a letter to Mr Brown, the Clerk to the City Council, saying why you and your friends support the coming of the factory. Pretend to be one of the people above – Mrs Green or Tom Stone, for instance.

4 When you have finished, form groups and select the best letter as you did before. Do the same as a class.

You have now learned another important point in presenting an argument. You have to understand the other points of view.

1 There are two sides to every argument.
2 It is quite fair to make your case stronger by pointing out the weak points in the opposite view.
3 State your case clearly and don't waste words.
4 Back up your case with facts and figures if you can. Give reasons why your case is stronger.
5 If you can, argue for a group, not just yourself.

The public enquiry

When people can't agree about something like a new building or where to put a factory, the Government sometimes orders a public enquiry. They appoint an Inspector who hears both sides of the argument and then decides what will happen.

The Government decided to hold a public enquiry.

What you do

Be the Inspector and write your report to the Government giving your decision. Write your report in four paragraphs like this:

In the first paragraph say what the argument is about (whether or not a factory should be built on Rushington Green). You should say a little about the green and what it is used for.
In your second paragraph put down all the arguments for the factory and why the City Council want to build it.
In the third paragraph give all the reasons local people have given against the factory.
In your last paragraph give your decision for or against and say why you gave that decision.

Don't discuss your decision with anyone. Make up your own mind. You have heard all the arguments.

When you have all finished writing your reports, take a class vote and see whether the factory will be built or not.

Rushington rumbles on

Some people in Rushington decided to appeal against the Inspector's decision. You can join in if you like.

Have a class debate about the factory – for and against.

Run a for-or-against campaign with badges and posters, pictures and pamphlets showing what the green will look like with a factory on it.

Use your tape recorder to tape interviews with Rushingtonians to get their opinions. Some may be undecided – the 'Don't Knows'.

Other ideas

When you have had enough of Rushington and its problems here are some other ideas that could start an interesting argument.

You will hear people saying these things. Will you argue for or against?

There will be other topics for you to debate and write about. Look in the local paper, especially the 'Letters to the Editor' section.

Unit 3 Writing poetry

Poems can be short . . .

The song of canaries

Never varies
And when they're moulting
They're pretty revolting.

. . . or even shorter:

Reflection on babies

A bit of talcum
Is always walcum.

These two short, comic verses are by Ogden Nash, a professional poet, but you don't have to be a real poet to enjoy writing poems.

Here is one by a very young boy in a primary school:

My teacher

Mrs Bond is nice, she shouts
and makes me jump
and when she says get
your sums book out I
nearly faint and when she
says put on your pumps I
think I run round the world
and across the playground
and when she says run I run and when
she says jump I jump.

Kevin Brown (aged six)

Writing verse can be fun. It can help us use words well. This unit will help you to express your feelings and ideas in an interesting way.

Odd odes

When the BBC's 'Blue Peter' programme ran an 'Odd Ode' contest 11,521 children entered. If 11,521 children can do it, so can you. Odd Odes aren't too hard to write. They are fun and make a good starting point for writing poetry.

This is the tale of Bertha Brown
Who had the biggest nose in town
One day while at her place of learning
She said 'Please Miss, there's something burning'.
You'd better tell old Farmer Brown
That his haystack's burning down.'
And sure enough two miles away,
They found a pile of smouldering hay.
Now Bertha's got her just rewards,
Her likeness will be in Tussauds.
The only reason for delay,
Her nose requires extra clay.

Andrew Ridley aged 7

Odd Odes were invented by the comedian Cyril Fletcher

Think of a funny name like Eli Scratcher or Septimus Starch.
Think of something unusual about the person. Write about something that happens to him or her.
The last line generally makes a special point.
Get the rhythm in your head – 'De dum de dum de dum de dum'.

What you do

1 Try writing your first ode:

This is the tale of Reginald Bark
Who would do anything for a lark,
One day . . .

(Now you finish it.)

2 Think of a funny name and write an ode of your own. Read your ode to the class after if you wish. Make a collection of the best, and illustrate and display them.

In Odd Odes the lines rhyme in pairs: first and second, third and fourth, etc. The rhyming pattern in poetry is important.

Limericks

Limericks are also quite easy to write once you get the idea.

There was an old man who said 'Do
Tell me how I can add two and two,
I think more and more
That it makes about four
But I fear that is almost too few.

Anon

Nobody knows who wrote that limerick. That's what Anon means – anonymous. Limericks are five lines long. Do you see how the rhythm goes?

Di dumity dumity dum,
Di dumity dumity dum,
Di dumity dum
Di dumity dum
Di dumity dumity dum.

The first line usually starts: 'There was a . . . ' and then the limerick goes on 'young man', or 'young girl', or 'old man', etc.

What you do

1 Write the last line of this limerick. The last line will tell us what happened to the girl from Madrid.

There was a young girl of Madrid
Who failed in whatever she did,
One day in the sky
She attempted to fly
And . . .

2 This time you only have two lines to help:

There was a young fellow of Caster,
Who tried to do everything faster,
. . . . etc.

3 Now you have the idea, write some limericks of your own. Share them with your friends. If you find writing limericks very hard, work in pairs. That will help.

Nonsense verse

The White Rabbit gives evidence to the court in Lewis Carroll's *Alice in Wonderland.* It doesn't make sense.

They told me you had been to her
And mentioned me to him:
She gave me a good character
But said I could not swim.

He sent them word I had not gone
(He know it to be true)
If she should push the matter on
What would become of you?

I gave her one, they gave him two
You gave us three or more
They all returned from him to you
Though they were mine before.

If I or she should chance to be
Involved in this affair,
He trusts to you to set them free
Exactly as we were.

The White Rabbit's verse isn't supposed to make sense. It is non-sense verse. Sometimes even the word s don't make sense. Look at Spike Milligan's 'Ning Nang Nong':

On the Ning Nang Nong,
Where the cows go Bong
And the Monkeys all say boo!
There's a Ning Nang Ning
Where the trees go Ping!
And the tea pots Jibber Jabber Joo.

What you do

1 Make a collection together as a class of some other nonsense verse. Look through any books in your library by Edward Lear, Lewis Carroll and Spike Milligan. Read and enjoy them together. It is more fun to laugh in company.

2 Try writing some nonsense verse yourself. You can use nonsense words like 'plink plank plonk' that just rhyme with other nonsense words, or use proper words and sentences that should make sense but don't – like the White Rabbit's evidence.

Serious poetry

Sometimes poets want to say something they feel is important.

My mother saw a dancing bear

My mother saw a dancing bear
By the school yard a day in June.
The keeper stood with a chain and bar
And whistle pipe, and played a tune.

And Bruin lifted up its head
And lifted its dusty feet,
And all the children laughed to see
It caper in the summer heat.

They watched as for the Queen it died.
They watched it march. They watched it halt.
They heard the keeper as he cried,
'Now roly-poly!' 'Somersault!'

And then my mother said, there came
The keeper with the begging cup,
The bear with burning coat of fur,
Shaming the laughter to a stop.

They paid a penny for the dance,
But what they saw was not the show;
Only, in Bruin's aching eyes,
Far-distant forests, and the snow.

Charles Causley

Take one home for the kiddies

On shallow straw, in shadeless glass
Huddled by empty bowls they sleep;
No dark, no dam, no earth, no grass –
'Mam get us one of those to keep'.

Living toys are something novel,
But it soon wears off somehow.
Fetch the shoebox, fetch the shovel –
'Mam we're playing funerals now'.

Philip Larkin

What you do

1 **Discussion time**
Read these two poems, first by yourself and then as a class. What do you think Charles Causley is saying about the bear? Is he saying something about people and animals? What is Philip Larkin saying about people and their pets? After your discussion, write what you think the poets are saying.

2 Poets like Charles Causley, Philip Larkin, John Walsh and Pam Ayres write for children as well as adults. Their poems often have a message for us. We have to look for it sometimes.
Find some of their poems and those of other poets to read. See what they have to say.

3 Try writing a poem about your own feelings or making a point you think important. It's not easy, but it isn't quite as hard as you might think at first.

Word pictures

Poets can draw us the most wonderful pictures in words.

Vulture

The vulture's very like a sack
Set down and left there drooping.
His crooked neck and creaky beak
Look badly bent from stooping.
Down to the ground to eat dead cows
So they won't go to waste,
Thus making up in usefulness
For what he lacks in taste.

X J Kennedy

Mrs McHingy

Old Mrs McHingy so drab and so dingy
Dressed all in black from her head to her toes.
She sits all alone in her old rocking chair
With her spectacles perched on her old beaky nose.
All by herself in her horrible kitchen
With no-one to talk to, not even a cat.
But 'Silence is golden' says Mrs McHingy,
So nobody ever drops in for a chat.

from *Mrs McHingy* by Diana Harland

Look at the next page for some help in making verse pictures yourself.

What you do

Poets often search a long time for just the right word.

1 Make sure with your teacher that you understand what adjectives and similes are.

2 Find the adjectives and similes used in 'Mrs McHingy' and 'The Vulture'. With your teacher think of some more similes and write them on the board.

3 Think hard and then write down two adjectives to go with each of these people if you were describing them. The first is done to help you start:

Coalman – black and dusty.
Nurse – . . . . and . . . .
Old lady – . . . . and . . . .
Punk – . . . . and . . . .
Pirate – . . . . and . . . .
Policeman – . . . . and . . . .

Choose some more people or animals and write two or more adjectives that could be used to describe them. It gets easier the more you practise.

4 Can you complete these similes?

The spaceman's helmet was like a . . .
The tramp's red nose shone like a . . .
The crocodiles lay on the river mud like . . .
Like a . . . . . . the mist rolled towards the ship.
As swift as . . . the native hurled his spear.

5 Imagine an Indian warrior in a Western film. He stands silently upon a hill watching a wagon train of pioneers wind slowly through the valley below. Think of the way he watches, his fierce face, keen eyes, the colour of his feathered head-dress, his tunic and weapons.

Try to write a short verse describing him as vividly as the poet describes Mrs McHingy. Aim first for a good description and then work it into rhyme and rhythm.

6 You may find writing this sort of poetry much harder than odes and limericks, but just do your best. Here are some more suggestions to try:

A great blue whale surfacing beside your ship.
An owl sitting on a branch in the moonlight.
The discovery of an old wreck by divers.
A rag and bone man's yard full of unusual things.
The last dragon.

You may think of some more people, animals or places to describe.

Odd Odes and limericks; comic verse and nonsense verse; word pictures and poems with a message. We can't all write great poetry, but we can all enjoy writing poems.

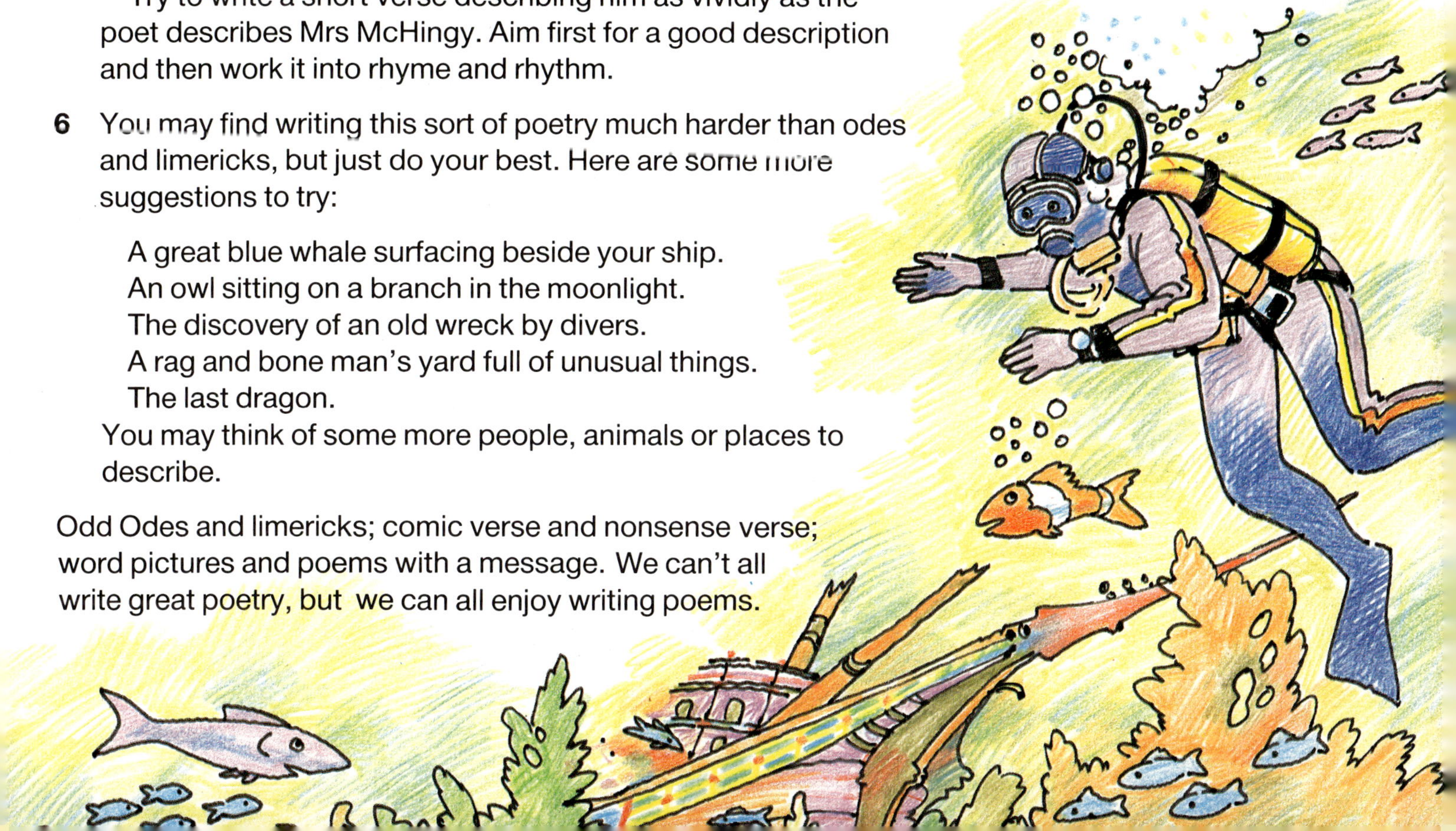

Writing is often used to try and persuade us to act or think in certain ways. We need to know when this is happening and what the writer is trying to do. This unit will help us understand this kind of writing.

Advertisements are all around us. They are a good example of persuasive writing, aimed at children and adults. They want us to:

TRY IT JOIN IT BUY IT VISIT IT SELL IT GIVE IT

Look at these three advertisements. They are all very different.

One helps someone in need. It is not intended to make money for the advertiser.
One can be helpful to us and is good business for the seller.
The third sort only helps the seller and can be actually harmful to us.

What you do

1 Decide which advert helps someone in need, which helps the seller and could be useful to us, and which one could be harmful to us.

2 **Discussion time**
Talk about the three types of advertisement above and find some other examples.

3 Make up three advertisements of your own:
- **a** One that helps a good cause;
- **b** One that sells a useful product;
- **c** One that is attractive but could be harmful.

4 **Discussion time**
How do advertisers try to make smoking attractive to people? Look at their advertisements and talk about them with your teacher.

Do advertisements tell the truth?

This picture is used by the Advertising Standards Authority.
The man in the mirror isn't very much like the real man.
It is against the law to tell lies in an advertisement.
The Advertising Standards Authority have to see that adverts tell the truth, not distort it like the mirror is doing.

Although it is unlikely that an advertisement will tell a deliberate lie, it does not have to tell us all the facts or give us all the information we should really have.

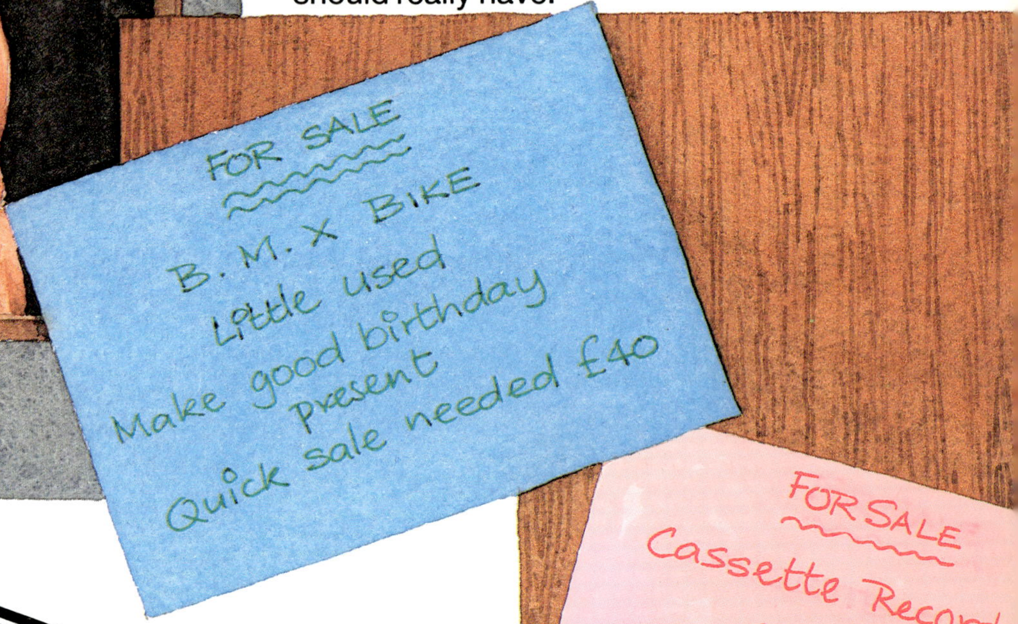

What you do

1 Look at these two advertisements. Do they tell us all we need to know about the bike and the cassette recorder?
Write down any questions you might like to ask before you bought these two items.

2 Write out an advertisement for some old toys that you want to sell.
You must tell all the facts about the broken spring, dents, scratches on the car, or the teddy's lost ear.
Look at your own advertisement and those of your friends. Do you think anyone will buy what you are selling, or even come to look?

Almost all the facts

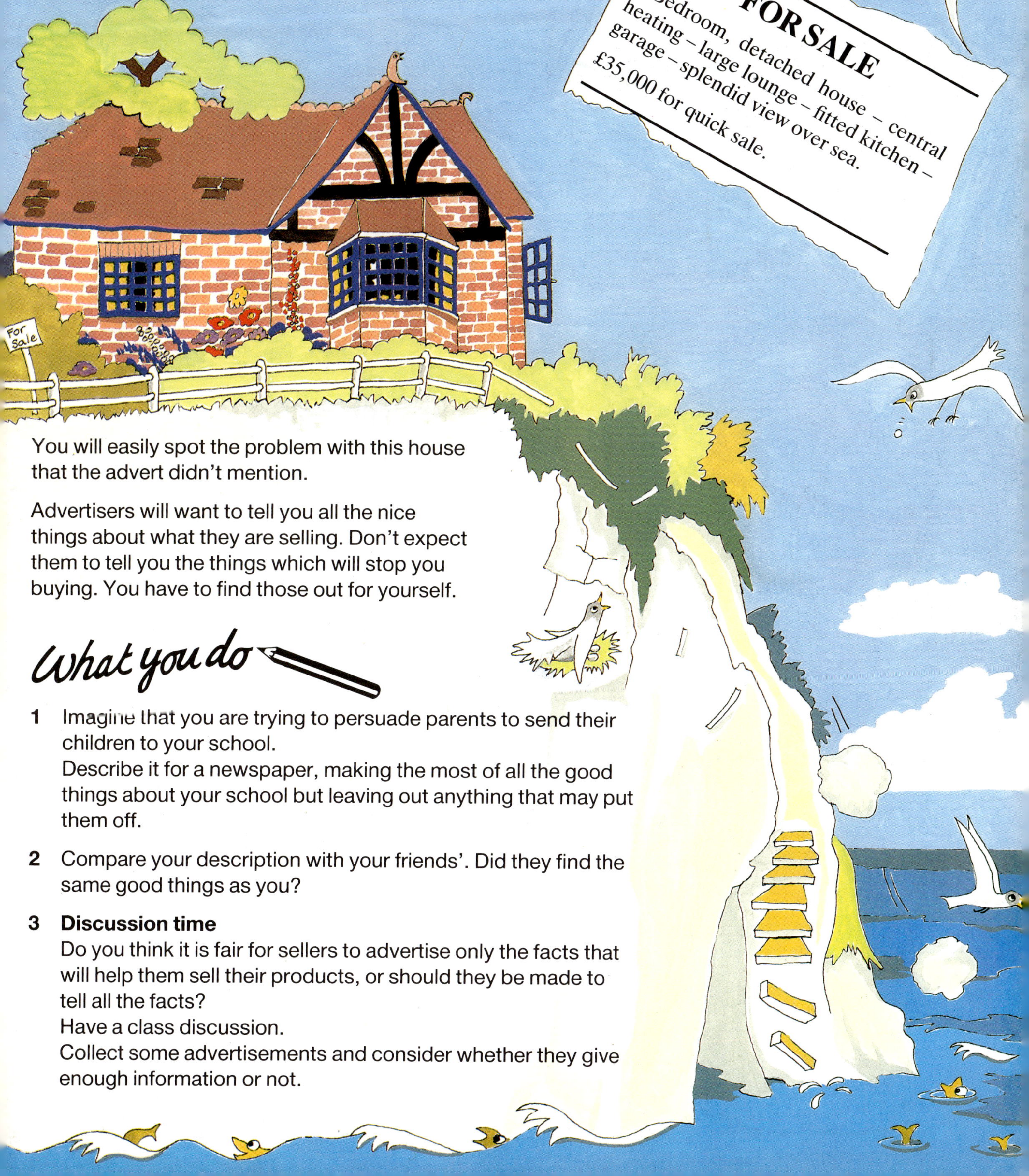

You will easily spot the problem with this house that the advert didn't mention.

Advertisers will want to tell you all the nice things about what they are selling. Don't expect them to tell you the things which will stop you buying. You have to find those out for yourself.

What you do

1 Imagine that you are trying to persuade parents to send their children to your school.
Describe it for a newspaper, making the most of all the good things about your school but leaving out anything that may put them off.

2 Compare your description with your friends'. Did they find the same good things as you?

3 **Discussion time**
Do you think it is fair for sellers to advertise only the facts that will help them sell their products, or should they be made to tell all the facts?
Have a class discussion.
Collect some advertisements and consider whether they give enough information or not.

Reaching people

Advertisers use all sorts of methods to get their advertisements noticed and to make us buy things.

What you do

1. Write down all the different ways that are used to bring advertisements in front of us: newspapers; magazines; radio, etc.
2. If you were an advertiser, what method would you use? Why?
3. Look at the advertisement for Maddocks' shop. What kinds of things persuade you to visit the shop soon?
   Look for advertisements in papers and magazines which are urging you to buy, give or sell right away. Make a collection.
4. Your class may like to finish this section on advertising by making a display illustrating some of the things you have learnt about advertising.

★ Advertisements can be useful, harmless or harmful.
★ Advertisements try to appear as if they were meant just for us. They are very personal.
★ Advertisements tell us the good things about a product – not the possible problems or weaknesses.
★ Advertisements try to make us want something. Often we don't really need it and could use our money in better ways.
★ We should always look for facts that we can be sure of in any advertisement or any other sort of persuasive writing.

A vote for Muriel

When elections for a Council or Parliament come around every four or five years, the candidates write to everyone in the area trying to persuade people to vote for them.

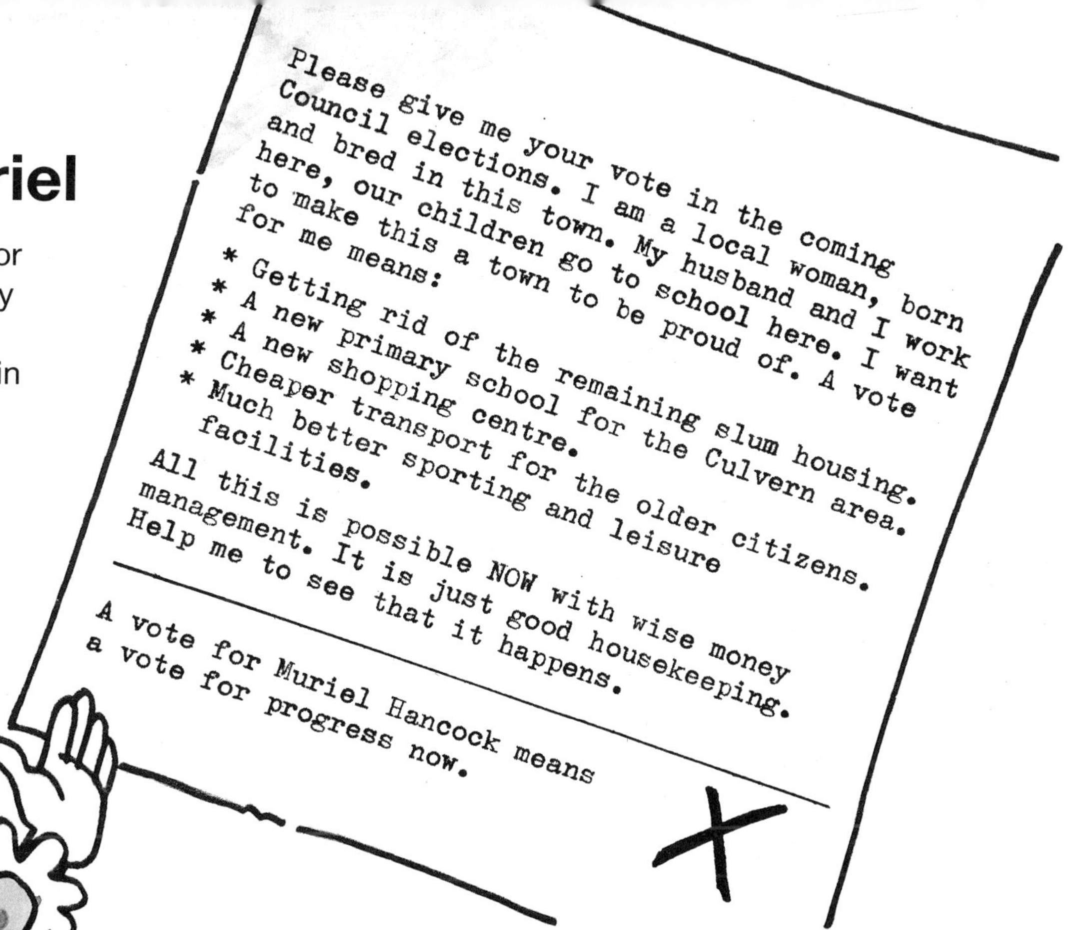

Please give me your vote in the coming Council elections. I am a local woman, born and bred in this town. My husband and I work here, our children go to school here. I want to make this a town to be proud of. A vote for me means:

* Getting rid of the remaining slum housing.
* A new primary school for the Culvern area.
* A new shopping centre.
* Cheaper transport for the older citizens.
* Much better sporting and leisure facilities.

All this is possible NOW with wise money management. It is just good housekeeping. Help me to see that it happens.

A vote for Muriel Hancock means a vote for progress now.

This pre-election letter is a very good example of 'persuasive' writing.
The candidate writes about all the good things she will do, the experience she has.
She tries to appeal to voters both young and old.
She promises to act 'NOW'.

What you do

1 Look at Muriel Hancock's letter to the voters. Discuss it and try to find all the different things she says to appeal to them. For instance, she says she is local. This means she will know what local people want. What is needed is good housekeeping. She claims to know about that. These are just examples. If you look carefully there are others.

2 Now it's your turn to write a letter to voters. Imagine your class is going to elect a class monitor. You would very much like the job. Write an election letter like the one above trying to persuade the class to vote for you.

Imagine you are going to stand for the Council. Write a letter like the one above and say all the good things you will do for the town.

Letters to the Editor

People often write to newspapers if they feel strongly about something. They hope to persuade other people to think as they do.

To the editor

Dear Sir,

I write to express my disgust at the shameful killing of a stag in the very centre of our town.

I am sure that many people were as angry as I was when the poor creature in its distress and fear ran into the car park and was finally cornered and killed by the so-called sportsmen who enjoy this dreadful pastime.

Is it not time that a law was passed to stop this cruel hunting of innocent and beautiful animals? Soon there will be no wildlife left in this over-crowded land of ours.

We shall all be the poorer then. I appeal to all who feel as I do to put pressure on the Government through their MP to stop this cruel hunting of deer.

Hazel Timothy (Mrs)

To the Editor

Dear Sir,

As Master of the Hunt I wish to reply to the letter from Mrs Timothy. We regret that the stag ran into the town centre. It was no fault of the hunt. No hounds were allowed into the town and two huntsmen dealt with the stag quickly and painlessly.

Mrs Timothy, like many other people, is quite wrong about hunting. There is no clear evidence that the sport is cruel. Deer have to be controlled or they do extensive damage to farmland. Shooting is far more likely to leave the animal wounded and in pain. This never happens with the hunt.

Finally, may I say that huntsmen are countrymen. They live in the country and do far more to protect it and its wildlife than those who live in towns.

Geoffrey Wilden
Master

What you do

A stag was killed in the middle of a town . . . it really did happen.

1 Write a letter to the paper supporting Mrs Timothy or Mr Wilden.

2 Discussion time
Does the class agree with hunting? Should all hunting be banned or just certain types? After all, fishing is hunting.

More ideas

Here are some more suggestions for ‘persuasive writing’.

What you do

1 You are going on holiday. Write to your best friend and try to persuade him or her to come with you.

2 You have just come to live in Britain. Write a letter to a friend back home persuading him or her to come and live here.

3 You have just seen a television programme on the dangers of smoking. You are writing a letter to your older brother who smokes heavily. You decide to include a paragraph trying to persuade him to stop.

4 Guy Fawkes tried to blow up Parliament. Write him a letter persuading him not to do it. Try to make him see the danger to himself and how dreadful it would be to kill all those people.

5 You want to hold a junior disco at your school. Write to the head teacher persuading him or her to let you have one.

6 A film company is making a picture in your town. They want some local children to act in it. Write to the director and tell him how suitable you think you are to take part. The film is about children stranded on another planet.

7 You want to join an exploration party to the Amazon Forest. How do you persuade the leader to take you?

8 You want to be the first child in space. Write to the Space Director to say why you think you are suitable.

9 Write another ‘Letter to the Editor’ on any subject you feel strongly about.

Military clampdown o
crashed mystery plan

A Quay welcom
for Greenpeace

Local heroes

Compromise o
tax cuts

Snags beset bid to scale Everest

Kiwis put to flight

Plea for traffic in metro report

Patients wait in cash crisis

Briefly . . .
Severn dam jobs chance

Newspaper reports are very important. They tell us what is going on in the world. They influence what people think and do. This unit helps you understand them and gives you a chance to write some for yourself.

The first thing we see are the headlines.

What you do

1. Which headline above caught your attention first?
   Can you think of the reasons why it caught your attention and write them down?
   Was it the size of the print? The words used? Was it short and catchy? Was it because it was about something that interested you?
2. Compare your choice with those of your friends. Did they make the same choice?
3. When you have talked about what makes a good headline, write two or three. Use items of news from school or the national or local news.

A good opening

After the headline the report often has a few words in heavy print. These introduce the main theme of the report – they tell us what the report is about and are called a **byline.**
The reporter uses lively language and doesn't waste words.

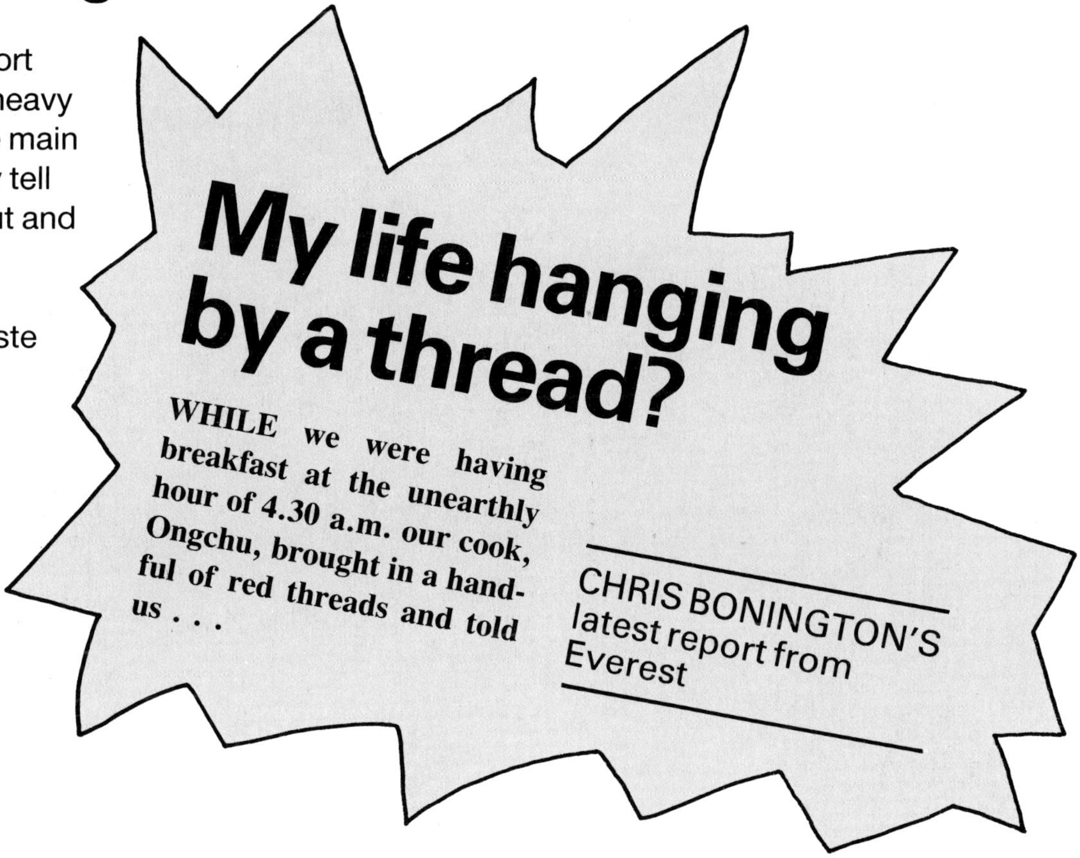

My life hanging by a thread?

WHILE we were having breakfast at the unearthly hour of 4.30 a.m. our cook, Ongchu, brought in a handful of red threads and told us . . .

CHRIS BONINGTON'S latest report from Everest

What you do

1 This was a good headline to Chris Bonington's report on his Mount Everest climb. The opening paragraph makes you want to read on and find out more about the 'red threads' the cook brought in.
Write down what you think makes this a good headline and start to the report. Can you guess what the 'red threads' were?

2 'Raise the Titanic'. That is the headline as the first efforts to lift the great liner from the bottom of the ocean begin. Write the opening paragraphs, including the headline and the byline, for this report. You could start something like this:

Dawn was breaking over a grey sea as the . . .

You carry on and write about eight lines of about eight words each.

Same news – different paper

The same news can be reported in very different ways – it depends on how that newspaper wants you to see the news.

Daily News

Fury over licence decision

Young people in the town are furious over the council's refusal to grant a late licence to the popular 'Full Moon Club', one of the town's few youth . . .

Daily Echo

Public welcome licence refusal

After many complaints of noise late at night, revving motor cycles and drunken shouts, the council have refused a late licence to the 'Full Moon Club'. Local residents welcomed the good news in many . . .

Newspapers must tell the truth – if they told lies people would soon stop buying them. But they are allowed to present the news in different ways. It is very important that we understand this when we read papers.

What you do

1 Work in pairs. You are reporters on rival newspapers. Each has a different policy on a new road the Government want to build.

The *Daily News* wants the road, which will bring new industry and more tourists to the area.
The *Daily Echo* says the road will cut through very beautiful countryside, spoil villages and so on. It wants the road to take another route, even though this will be more expensive and take longer.

Each write a headline and report on the day the Government says a road is to be built.

2 Make a class collection of newspapers on one day and see how the same news is presented in different papers.

Remember Jack, the hero of *Jack and the Beanstalk?*

Do you remember the story of how he climbed the beanstalk and found a giant's castle at the top, and how he stole the hen that laid the golden egg?
When the giant chased him he cut down the beanstalk and destroyed the giant, his wife and his castle.

We are always on Jack's side in the story; after all, the giant was going to eat him.

But
Suppose you were writing the story for the *Giant Weekly.* What sort of headline would you have? What sort of report would you expect?

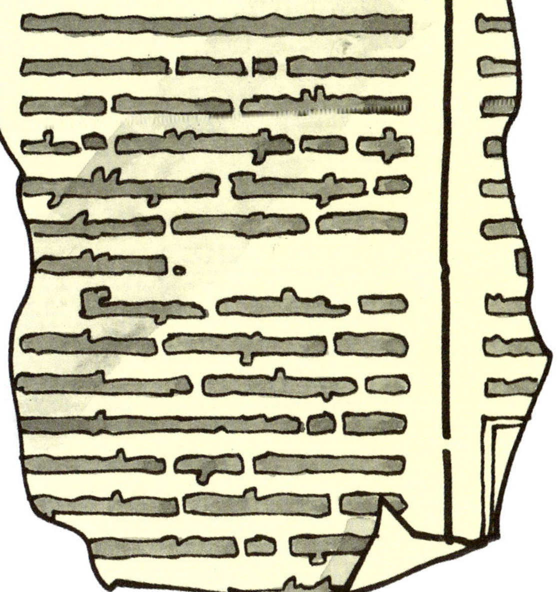

What you do

1 Finish writing the report for *Giant Weekly.* Write out the start above first.

2 Write headlines and short reports for:
The *Moon Times* published by the inhabitants of the moon when Neil Armstrong and the first Earth ship landed.
The *Red Indian Journal* after yet another wagon train of settlers arrive in Indian country and start to drive out the inhabitants.
The *Witches' Weekly* after Gretel trapped the Witch of the Gingerbread House in her own oven.
The *Spanish Echo* after Sir Francis Drake and the English fleet defeated the Armada.
The *Nottingham Norman News* the day after another attack on wealthy travellers in Sherwood Forest by the outlaw Robin Hood.

The Pied Piper

The legend of the Pied Piper is one of the strangest stories ever told. You are going to be a reporter telling your readers what happened – as it happened.

This is the way the headlines may have looked if there had been newspapers in 1376 in the little German town of Hamelin. The town had been invaded by thousands of rats – rats – rats – rats – rats – rats . . .

In 1376 Hamelin suffered a plague of rats. They were everywhere: eating food, killing cats, biting babies. No-one could get rid of them, life was a misery. Then one day a strangely dressed man with a pipe appeared. He played it and all the rats followed him and were swept away by the river. But the foolish mayor refused to pay him and the citizens laughed at him.

Again the Piper played his magic pipe and this time all the children followed him. He led them out of the town to the side of a mountain where a great opening appeared. Watched by all the people, who were unable to move, the Piper and the children entered the mountain and disappeared for ever.

Robert Browning has written a wonderful poem about this story called *The Legend of the Pied Piper.* If you can, read it together before you start the questions.

The First Report

July 20th 1376

You are a reporter sent to cover the strange invasion of rats in Hamelin Town for the Brunswick Times.

Rats!
They fought the dogs and
killed the cats,
And bit the babies in their cradles,
And ate the cheese out of the vats,
And licked the soup from the cooks' own ladles,
Split open the kegs of salted sprats,
Made nests inside men's Sunday hats,
And even spoilt the women's chats,
By drowning their speaking
With shrieking and squeaking
In fifty different sharps and flats.

from *The Pied Piper of Hamelin* Robert Browning

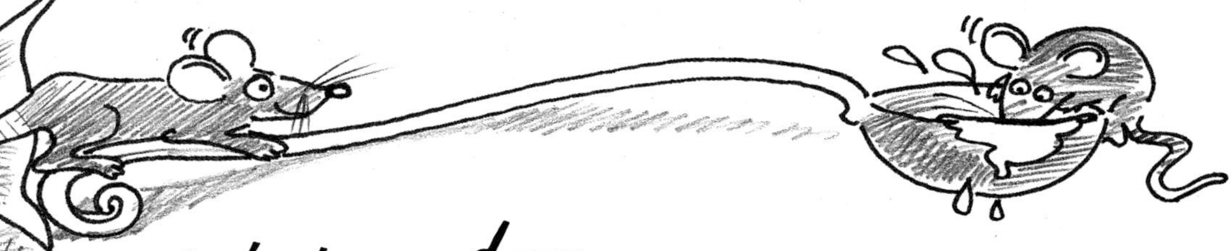

What you do

The date is July 20th 1376. You send off your first report on the rats in Hamelin. A headline and a start to your report is suggested for you, but you need not use them if you don't wish to.

Write a really exciting report on the damage the rats are doing and the state of the people. A little of Browning's poem is quoted to help you imagine what it was like. Draw pictures with your report.

The Second Report

July 22nd 1376

The Piper has appeared, played his pipe and cleared the rats. The townspeople are overjoyed; the Piper is a hero.

Into the street the Piper stept,
Smiling first a little smile,
As if he knew what magic slept
In his quiet pipe the while;
Then like a musical adept,
To blow his pipe his lips were wrinkled,
And green and blue his sharp eyes twinkled,
Like a candle-flame where salt is sprinkled;
And ere three shrill notes the pipe uttered,
You heard as if an army muttered;
And the muttering grew to a grumbling;
And the grumbling grew to a mighty rumbling;
And out of the houses the rats came tumbling.
Great rats, small rats, lean rats, brawny rats,
Brown rats, black rats, grey rats, tawny rats,
Grave old plodders, gay young friskers,
Fathers, mothers, uncles, cousins,
Cocking tails and prickling whiskers,
Families by tens and dozens,
Brothers, sisters, husbands, wives –
Followed the piper for their lives.
From street to street he piped advancing,
And step by step they followed dancing,
Until they came to the River Weser,
Wherein all plunged and perished!
– Save one, who stout as Julius Caesar,
Swam across and lived to carry
To Rat-land home his commentary.

What you do

The date is July 22nd. Write your report to the paper describing the coming of the strangely dressed Piper, his magic pipe and the great rejoicing in the town as the rats are cleared.
Once again there is a headline and the start of your report to use if you wish, and some splendid lines from Robert Browning's poem to give you ideas about what it was like as the rats followed the Piper.

The Third Report

later on July 22nd

It is late in the afternoon. The Mayor has refused to pay the Piper as he promised and tragedy has struck the town.

Read the poem, from this point to the end, together as a class, if you can find the text of it in a book.

Once more he stept into the street
And to his lips again
Laid his pipe of smooth straight cane;
And ere he blew three notes . . .
There was a rustling,
That seemed like a bustling,
Of merry crowds justling
at pitching and hustling,
Small feet were pattering,
wooden shoes clattering,
Little hands clapping and
Little tongues chattering,
And like fowls in a farmyard
when barley is scattering,
Out came the children running
All the little boys and girls
With rosy cheeks and flaxen curls,
And sparkling eyes and teeth like pearls,
Tripping and skipping, ran merrily after
The wonderful music with shouting and laughter.

The Mayor was dumb, and the Council stood,
As if they were changed into blocks of wood,
Unable to move a step or cry
To the children merrily skipping by.

What you do

The Piper has blown his pipe to terrible effect.
Write a special report to your paper describing the Mayor's action, the Piper drawing all the children from the town, the desperate attempts of the townsfolk to get into the mountain, their anger at the Mayor.
You have a suggested headline and some lines from the poem to help.

More ideas

No-one really knows quite what happened 600 years ago in Hamelin town. But there really is a stone pillar, telling the story, on the mountainside just outside the town and in the church at Hamelin is a great stained glass window showing the Piper and the children.

What you do

1 Write a report on the town in the days following the children's disappearance. Did the Mayor make amends or excuse his action?
Did they search for the children?

2 Write up an interview you have had with the little lame boy who was left behind, what the Piper's music promised and how he is without any friends.

3 **Either** Imagine you were one of the children and write about the wonderful land the Piper led you to on the other side of the mountain.
Or You could be a reporter who found the children years after.

4 You track down and interview the Piper years later. How does he feel about his actions now?

5 Papers have to give just facts in their reports. If they want to give an opinion they have to put it in an 'Opinion' or 'Editorial Comment' column.
Write your opinion on the happenings. Who was to blame? The Mayor? Did the Piper act badly or the citizens? Are you sorry for the parents?

6 Act out a town meeting between the Mayor, his council and the citizens who are very angry. Some of you be reporters and write up what happens.

You should know now how to write a newspaper report. Find some interesting events in school, your town or in the national news to report.

Unit 6 Taking notes

Writing notes is a very important skill.

Students use it, children in school use it, reporters use it, office workers use it, people in factories and shops use it. Writing notes helps most people remember better what they have seen, heard or read about.

This unit will help you learn how to take notes.

There has been a fire in town.
The reporter has been watching and taking notes.
When he gets back he writes up his report from his notes.

Near tragedy in town centre fire

A fierce fire raged through a house in the town centre last night. 25 Silver Street was quickly alight and by 10.05, only five minutes after the fire was reported, the brigade arrived. Flames were already reaching the top floor of the house when . . .

What you do

Finish writing the report using the notes that the reporter made on his writing pad.

Abbreviations, signs and symbols

Reporters, secretaries, typists and other people who have to take notes use **shorthand,** a special sort of note taking. It is too difficult for you to learn now, but here are some other suggestions to make note-taking easier.

Learn what the word **abbreviation** means.

What you do

1 Some abbreviations are worth learning by heart. Do you know what these mean?

Make as full a list as you can with your teacher.

2 You can make your own abbreviations by taking the vowels – a, e, i, o, u – out of words and still understand what the word means.
Make up some more abbreviations by taking out vowels.

could = cld   part = prt   should = shld   come = cme

3 There are lots of signs and symbols that are useful in note taking.
Find out what these signs mean.

> <   ←   ∴   &   ,,
=   →   ∵   v.   c.

Find as many of these sort of signs as you can. Invent some.

P.O.   R.S.P.C.A.   Y.H.A.   N.S.P.C.C.
U.K.   N.Z.   B.B.C.   H.Q.

4 Using initial letters can save writing time. The ones above are used a lot. Find out what the initial letters above stand for.
Find some more.

Here's a chance to practise using the signs, symbols and abbreviations you have just learnt.

Spy puzzle

With Captain Cook

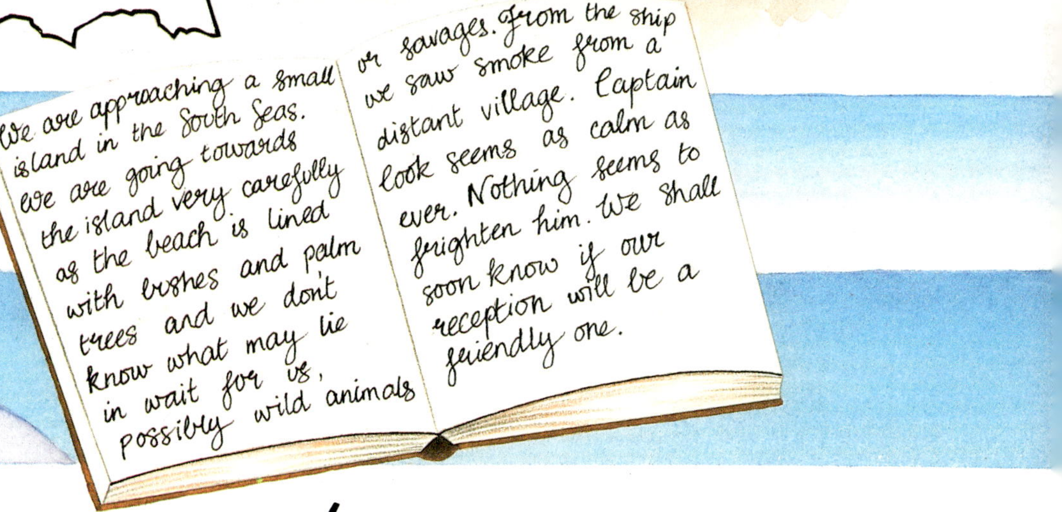

What you do

1 The spy has been watching an enemy camp. Unfortunately he has been captured but has managed to leave you his notebook. The message is urgent – you have to work out what it says.

2 You are a reporter on the ship of the great explorer Captain Cook.
You have just written up your report of a landing on an island. Put the report into notebook language like the spy's notes.

3 Your notes are just for you and usually you are the only person who needs to be able to read them. Just for fun, write some abbreviated notes on an event real or imaginary. Pass them to your friend and see if she can make sense of them and write a full report from them.

Observation

The secret of writing good notes is to watch carefully and listen carefully.
Try not to miss anything if you can help it.

We can practise good observation right here in our classroom.
There is something happening all the time, even when everything seems still and quiet.

What you do

1 Observe what goes on in your classroom for five minutes. Watch carefully and write your notes up like this:

10.00 Everyone quiet, can even hear people breathing.
10.02 Teacher stands, goes to the window, looks out.
10.03 David drops his pencil, laughs. Teacher looks at him.
10.04 Large bee comes in the window. Teacher sits down at desk.

Your notes will be different from these, of course. Use abbreviations.
If you have a watch or classroom clock, note the times.

2 When you have done your five minutes' observation and note-taking, write up your report like this:

> Five quiet minutes in Class Four
>
> Today we spent five minutes observing what happened in our classroom. At first nothing seemed to happen and then . . .

3 Discussion time
Compare your notes with your friends'. Did they spot something you missed? Try the exercise again on another day.

4 Before the next lesson spend a little while observing . . .
A street outside your house.
Your garden or backyard for birds, cats, people, insects.
The school playground.
A room inside your house.
Any other interesting place.

Take your notes and write your report during the next lesson.

People talking

Taking notes of what people say when you are:
having a lesson
when you interview someone
trying to learn from an educational programme on TV
is quite difficult, but you can do it if you practise.

What you do

1 Listen to a short discussion between your teacher and one of your classmates. They choose a familiar subject like 'What is your favourite game?' or 'The holiday I would most like' – something easy to talk about. You listen and as they talk you jot down notes on what they are talking about. It must be a short discussion.

Don't try to write each word.
Give some idea of what each one said.
Use abbreviations (T for teacher, S for Susan, etc.).

Remember you are not trying to record a conversation, just noting the main points being made.

2 Watch a TV or video programme together as a class or group. It should be a programme giving information, like a travel film or nature documentary. As the programme goes on take notes on the main theme to remind you of what it was about. After the programme, write up your notes – do it right after the programme. Later, you will be able to leave a longer time between your notes and your report.

Taking notes from people talking is quite hard, but don't be discouraged – you will improve gradually.

Using a tape recorder

Tape recorders are often used instead of notebooks.

For commentaries

What you do

Arrange to watch an event like a football or netball match, sports day or other school event, with two friends. Record a few minutes commentary each; don't try the whole match. Listen to your playback, discuss which sounded best and write up a report on that part of the match.

For interviews

Whether you use a tape recorder or a notebook, you will get better interviews if you:

Prepare by finding out a little about the person and your subject;
Prepare your questions;
Arrive on time and thank the person you are interviewing;
Get them talking before you start recording. Get used to each other;
Be patient. Thank them for helping you when you finish.

What you do

1 Select someone interesting to interview about their work or hobby:
  School staff – teachers, cooks, cleaners.
  Visitors to school – doctors, nurses, piano tuners, delivery men, policemen.
  Older relatives or friends.
  Friends' parents or relatives from other countries.
  People helpful to your project.

2 Try a make-believe interview. Your friends play the part of pop stars, famous people in history, space travellers or people from other countries which have problems.

  Write a little on what you learned from your interview.

Is this man being fair?
Could he justify what he is saying, prove it to be true?
It is often easier to say things like this than justify them.

This unit shows us that if we want to be fair we have to be able to justify what we say.

What you do

1 Make sure you understand what 'justify' means. It comes from the word 'justice'. It means being able to prove what you say or believe is fair or just. Talk about it with your teacher.

2 Do you think the man in the picture could justify what he says about lady drivers, foreigners, young people and so on?
Think of some other things that people often say that would be hard to justify. Is there any truth at all in what the man is saying?
Why do people say such things?

Have a *Discussion time* about this and then write what you think.

Hard and easy

Being able to justify what we do or allow to happen is even more important than justifying what we say.

Some things are easy to justify.

But some things are harder to justify.

Some things, such as having crossing places for people on busy roads, are easy to justify. It is a little hard to justify making animals do tricks in the circus, but many people feel it to be quite all right.

What you do

Read the list below. You may think some of the statements are justifiable, while some are not. Try to justify those you agree with and say why you disagree with the others.

People should not smoke in public places like a bus or cinema.
Animals should not be used to do tricks in the circus.
Birds in cages are quite content.
Vandals should be made to repair damage and clear up the mess they make.
Everyone should have to retire at 60 to make more jobs for young people.
We should stop spending money on space travel and use it for medical research.

Day dreaming

Mary, dreaming, far away – her eyes on
Ships and distant lands of bright birds in
Light crossed jungles.
Cities of shining spires and casement windows
Open to spiced breezes of the East.
  'Stay in at break,' Sir said,
  Bursting the bubble.

The afternoon was sunny and the classroom warm. Mary felt sleepy. Yesterday evening her sailor Dad had come back after a year away from home. Everyone had stayed up late talking. It was after 12 o'clock when Mary went to bed.

Mr Smart was explaining something very patiently, but Mary's mind was far away dreaming about the countries her Dad had talked of, with their white cities, high mountains and people who spoke different languages.

Suddenly the teacher's voice broke into her dream. 'Mary, for the last time, will you answer my question?' Mary looked blank – she hadn't heard a word.

'Right, young lady, stay in at break time and copy what I have written off the board.' Mary, her dreams quite shattered, sighed.

What you do

1 Do you think Mr Smart acted fairly? Was he justified in punishing Mary? Was there another way he could have acted? How would you have acted if you had been Mr Smart? Write what you think.

2 Imagine you are Mary. Write out what you would say to Mr Smart to excuse missing the question. Was anyone else to blame?

3 Have you ever been punished at school or at home and thought the punishment was unfair? Write about what happened and how you felt. When you have finished share your story with your friends.

Time change

Some things which were justifiable years ago would not be allowed now.

There are still plenty of people alive today who were born in Queen Victoria's reign. Your parents' grandfathers or grandmothers, perhaps even your grandparents may have been born when she was Queen. It wasn't very long ago, but . . .

In Victorian times you could still be sent to prison in Australia, or even hung for stealing a sheep.

In America slaves were still kept on cotton plantations.

In Britain women had no vote and all they owned belonged to their husbands. Very few girls went to school.

As years pass people change their minds about things – attitudes change.

What you do

1 **Discussion time**
Have a class discussion and try to think of other ways in which our attitudes have changed. For example, the treatment of children, animals and people who are mentally ill has changed greatly since Victorian times. Find out a little about the 19th century and see how attitudes have changed.

2 Why do you think people change their minds about what is fair? Is it because we are better educated, know more about what goes on?

3 Imagine you are a Victorian. Write how you would justify:
- Children working in mines.
- No votes for women.
- Dog fighting.
- Hanging someone for stealing a sheep.
- Man traps for poachers.

You won't find it easy to justify these things, but people did, not so long ago.

Fair-Unfair

Britain is a much better and fairer place to live in for most people than it was in Queen Victoria's reign.

The battery hen

Oh, I am a battery hen,
On me back there's not a germ,
I never scratched a farmyard,
And I never pecked a worm,
I never had the sunshine,
To warm me feathers through;
Eggs I lay, every day,
For the likes of you.

But it's no life for a battery hen,
In me box I'm sat,
A funnel stuck out from the side,
Me pellets come down that,
I gets a squirt of water,
Every half a day,
Watching with me beady eye,
Me eggs roll away.

I might have been a farmyard hen,
Scratching in the sun,
There might have been a crowd of chicks,
After me to run,
There might have been a cockerel fine
To pay us his respects,
Instead of sittin' here,
Till someones comes and wrings our necks.

Pam Ayres

There are still many things that some people think are fair and others think are unfair. We have to make up our own minds about them. Pam Ayres has made up her mind about battery hens, it seems.

What you do

1 We all eat eggs. They are kept cheap by battery farming. The hens are well fed and warm. So the battery farmer may argue. What do you think? Is battery hen farming justified or not? Write what you think and why.

2 Do you think people are kinder to animals and to other people than they used to be? You have found out in your history lessons about the way people used to act. What do you think?

A warm welcome

People are much more likely to be unfair to one another when they don't really know each other.

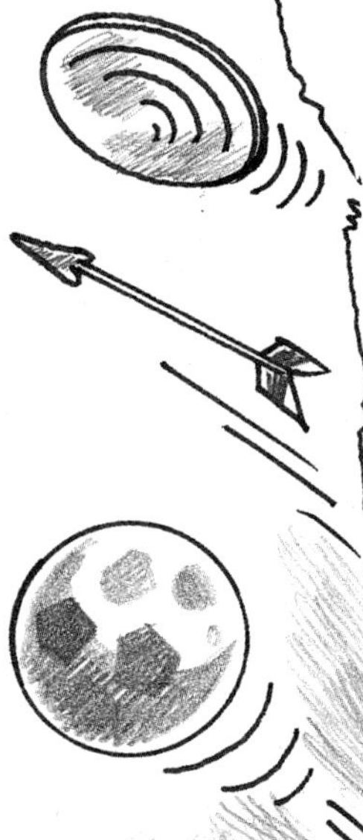

Strangers in the street

Kipling Street was a quiet street. The people were friendly when they met, but generally they looked after their houses and small gardens and kept themselves to themselves. There were only two or three children in the street, very little traffic and a small shop on the corner. It was a sleepy, pleasant place – on a Sunday morning you could almost hear a pin drop on the pavement.

Then the Ashtons moved in. Life was never the same again.

Mr and Mrs Ashton had five children and a granny. People in the street soon knew that things had changed. To begin with there was the noise. It was terrible. Mr Ashton loved old cars and he seemed to spend most of his time hammering and revving up engines. He was so keen on his hobby that he would often be still hammering and revving late at night.

The eldest boy, Kevin, had a motor bike that never seemed to be switched off. Mr Robinson, next door, said that he must take it to bed with him.

Mrs Ashton loved the radio and played it loud enough in the kitchen to be heard all over the house. Mrs Robinson said she could hear it in the corner shop.

The four younger children seemed to live in the garden or the street playing noisy games and shrieking with laughter. At 8.30 each morning they exploded into the street on their way to school leaping, laughing, shouting and swinging school bags at each other.

Worst of all was Granny Ashton, who was very fond of walking but rather forgetful. She often marched into the wrong house, sat down and demanded a cup of tea.

It was all too much for the neighbours. The noise, granny, children's grinning faces over garden walls, flying balls, arrows and frisbees. The family didn't fit even though they were a friendly lot and no-one had come to any real harm. The neighbours held a meeting and decided to write to Mr and Mrs Ashton.

Coping with the Ashtons

What are the Kipling Street folk going to do about the Ashtons?

What you do

1 The people of Kipling Street have asked you to write a letter to Mr Ashton complaining of the noise, behaviour, granny and the rest.

You write it and justify your complaints. Remember no-one has been hurt and the Ashtons are very friendly.

2 Now you are Mr Ashton. Write your reply. Try to justify the way you have acted. You haven't found the neighbours very friendly.

3 **Discussion time**
Were the Ashtons all to blame? Could their neighbours have acted differently? What can be done now to make things better?

Code of Conduct

No-one bothered to make the Ashtons welcome. It can happen in school to new boys and girls, especially if they are shy, speak or dress differently, or maybe have a handicap like deafness.

What can you do to make sure new children are welcome in your class?

What you do

Try writing a Code of Conduct to welcome new pupils to your class. It might read something like this:

> Class 2 welcomes new pupils
>
> We ask the teacher always to tell us if she knows a new boy or girl is coming.
>
> If we can, we find out a little bit about them, where they are coming from, how old they are, etc.
>
> When they arrive, we make sure . . .

Now you complete the code of welcome.

When you have all made up your own code, have a discussion. Draw up a really good one and put it up in your classroom.

Unit 8 Writing to reflect

Sometimes people say 'I haven't had time to think'. That's a pity. We all need time to stop and think – even children.

This unit is about stopping to think – to reflect – and writing down some of your thoughts.

Do you ever think about . . .

Grass

Do you ever think about grass
On the lawns that you pass?
The green of it,
The sheen of it,
The after raining clean of it
When it sparkles like glass?

Do you know what grass is,
Those green spears showing
Wherever you're going?

Every blade, to be brief,
Is a leaf
Without a twig, without a bough.
You never thought lawn mowers
Went around
Clipping leaves off the ground,
Did you now?

Aileen Fisher

What you do

Here are some questions to think, write and talk about.

1 What are the best things about being young? Perhaps it is not having to look after the house, get the meals, go out to work. Perhaps it is being able to play and have long holidays or being looked after. What do you think?

2 What are the worst things about being young? Being bossed about? Having to go to bed early? Not being allowed to watch some TV programmes? What else?

3 Can adults really remember what it was like to be a child? Do they imagine they were better than they were: better behaved, better mannered, quieter and so on? In what ways are they sometimes unfair to you?

When I was your age, child,
When I was eight,
When I was ten,
When I was two
(How old are you?)
When I was your age, child,
My father would have gone quite wild
Had I behaved the way you
Do

What! Food uneaten on my plate
When I was eight?
What! Room in such a filthy state
When I was ten?
What! Late
For school when I was two?
My father would have shouted, 'When
I was your age, child',
My father would have raved,
Had I behaved
The way you
Do.

When I was your age, child, I
Should never have dreamed
Of sitting idly
Watching television half the night.
It would have seemed
Demented:
Television not then having been
Invented.

So grow up child! And be
Your age. (What is your age then?)
Eight? Or nine? Or two or ten?
Remember when you look at me
When I was your age I was forty-three.

from *When I was your age* by Michael Frayn

4 Discussion time
What do you think Michael Frayn's last line means? Try to work it out as a class.

5 Peter Pan was a boy who never grew older; he stayed a boy. Would you like that? Or are you keen to grow up as soon as possible? Write about what you think.

6 What makes a person grow up? Apart from being bigger and stronger, how are grown-ups different from children? How are you different from when you were five, or even two? Ask some questions at home about yourself.

Do you ever think about **being old?**

'You are old, Father William,' the young man said,
'And your hair has become very white;
And yet you incessantly stand on your head –
Do you think, at your age, this is right?'

'In my youth' Father William replied to his son,
'I feared it might injure my brain;
But, now that I'm perfectly sure I have none,
Why, I do it again and again.'

'You are old,' said the youth, 'and your jaws are too weak
for anything tougher than suet.
Yet you finished the goose, with the bones and the beak;
Pray how do you manage to do it?'

'In my youth' said his father, 'I took to the law
And argued each case with my wife;
And the muscular strength that it gave to my jaw
Has lasted the rest of my life.'

'You are old,' said the youth, 'one would hardly suppose
That your eye was as steady as ever;
Yet you balance an eel on the end of your nose –
What makes you so awfully clever?'

'I have answered three questions, and that is enough'
Said his father; 'Don't give yourself airs.
Do you think I can listen all day to such stuff?
Be off, or I'll kick you downstairs.'

Lewis Carroll

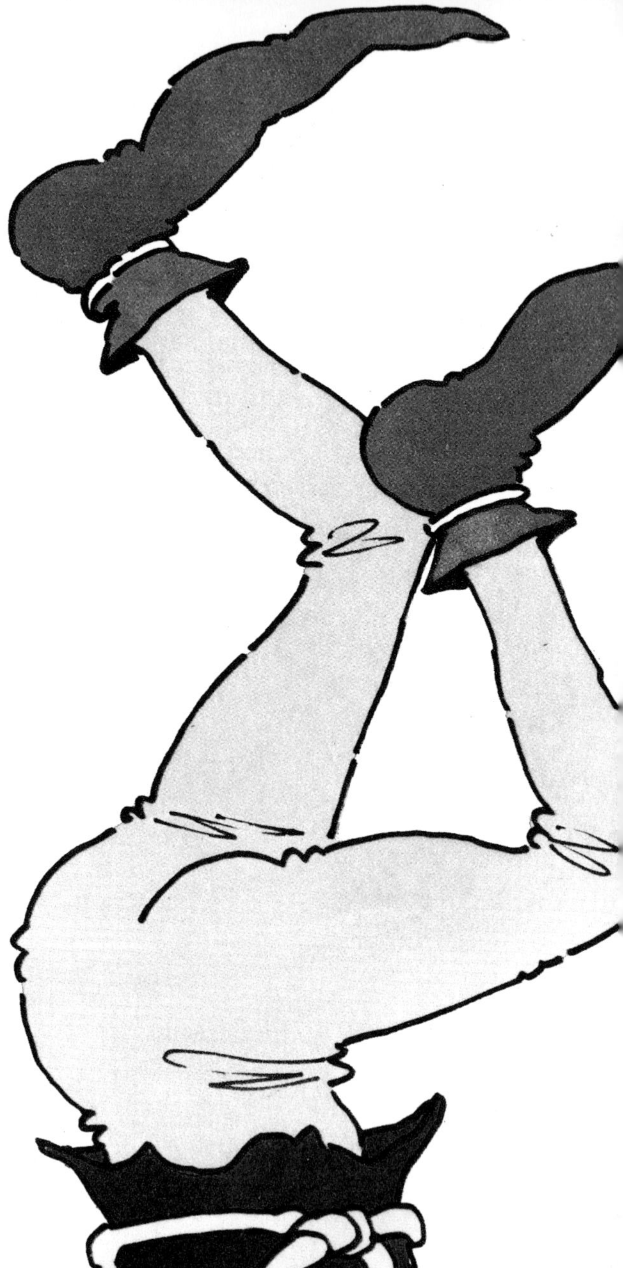

We all have to try and live together happily – young, middle aged and old. It helps if we reflect sometimes how other age groups feel and why they act as they do.

Father William did some very unusual things, didn't he? Not many old people balance eels on their noses or stand on their heads. But most of them are jolly interesting to know.

What you do

Here are some questions to think, write and talk about.

1 What is old? 40 years, 70 or 90 years old? People live longer, fitter lives now, so when are we old?

2 Are there things you can't do when you are old? Think about some elderly people you know. What do they find difficult?

3 Are there nice things about being old? Some people enjoy having more spare time, for instance. Think of some others.

4 Living a long time means you have had lots of different experiences. Do you think this makes old people wise?

5 If they are retired from work, but fit and active, how can older people help others – young and old? What sort of skills do they have that could be useful in society?

6 It is said that the very old and the very young understand each other. Is this true? What do they have in common?

7 People live to be a hundred years old sometimes. Have a class discussion about all the changes they have seen. Then imagine you are 100 years old, being interviewed by a reporter. Tell him about the changes you have seen.

8 Find an elderly person willing to talk to your class about the changes she has seen in her lifetime.

Do you ever think about **learning to care?**

This is the tale of Ethel Dare,
Who said she simply didn't care
If her town was daubed by vandals
Or the countryside was mangled,
If the seas were filled with litter
Or chimneys made the rainfall bitter.
She wouldn't help to find solutions
To the problems of pollution,
She didn't care about the hungry
Or the sick or sad or lonely,
Ethel thought the thing to do,
Was concentrate on 'ME' not 'YOU'.

It shouldn't come as a surprise,
When Ethel died that no-one cried.

People like Ethel are selfish. They make the world a less pleasant place to live in. We should try to make it a better place.

Are you learning to care more as you grow older? It is worth thinking about.

What you do

1 We should try to be caring towards everyone, but there may be some people who need our special care – like the sick, hungry or very young. Write a list of the sorts of people who may need our special care. Write a little about each group saying why they need our care and what you think we should be doing to help them.

2 Write down how you think you have been helpful to someone recently. How do you think you can help in the future?

3 Is your class or your school doing anything just now to help people in need? If not, why not organize an event (a sale, competition, a game, a collection) to raise money for some good cause?

4 Find out a little about organizations that help people in your town. These are often voluntary; the helpers are not paid.

It is not only people who need your help.

If we don't control factories our skies will be filled with chemicals which turn the rain acid. The acid rain causes forests to die and poisons rivers and lakes in neighbouring countries.

Too much refuse and waste material is being poured into the sea. Some seas like the Mediterranean are now very polluted.

Woodlands and hedges are rapidly being removed from our countryside. In Britain, over half the broadleaf woodlands have disappeared since 1945. This affects the look of the countryside and the homes of many animals and birds.

Some of our buildings, streets, playgrounds, parks and gardens are spoilt by vandalism and paint daubing.

What you do

1 Which of these problems do you think is most urgent? Which would you solve first? Write what you think could be done to solve that problem. You may like to work in groups on each problem. Discuss your ideas as a class when you have finished.

2 Find out about organizations which are trying to save woodlands, stop litter, save animals, improve our towns, and so on. There are a great many. Send for their pamphlets. Mount them in a 'We Care' corner with information from those that try to care for people.

3 Your class may like to do a project called 'Caring for our world'. Find out more about the dangers to our environment and how to fight them.

Write articles, design badges and posters, make models and maps to illustrate the dangers, write letters for a paper, paint pictures, interview people, write stories.

Do you remember your first day at school?

First day at school

A millionbillionwillion miles from home
Waiting for the bell to go. (To go where?)
Why are they all so big, other children?
So noisy? So much at home they
must have been born in uniform.
Lived all their lives in playgrounds
Spent the years inventing games
that don't let me in. Games
that are rough, that swallow you up.

And the railings.
All around, the railings.
Are they to keep out wolves and monsters?
Things that carry off and eat children?
Things you don't take sweets from?
Perhaps they're to stop us getting out
Running away from the lessins. Lessin.
What does a lessin look like?
Sounds small and slimy.
They keep them in glassrooms.
Whole rooms made out of glass. Imagine.

I wish I could remember my name
Mummy said it would come in useful.
Like wellies. When there's puddles.
Yellowwellies. I wish she was here.
I think my name is sewn on somewhere
Perhaps the teacher will read it for me.
Tea-cher. The one who makes the tea.

Roger McGough

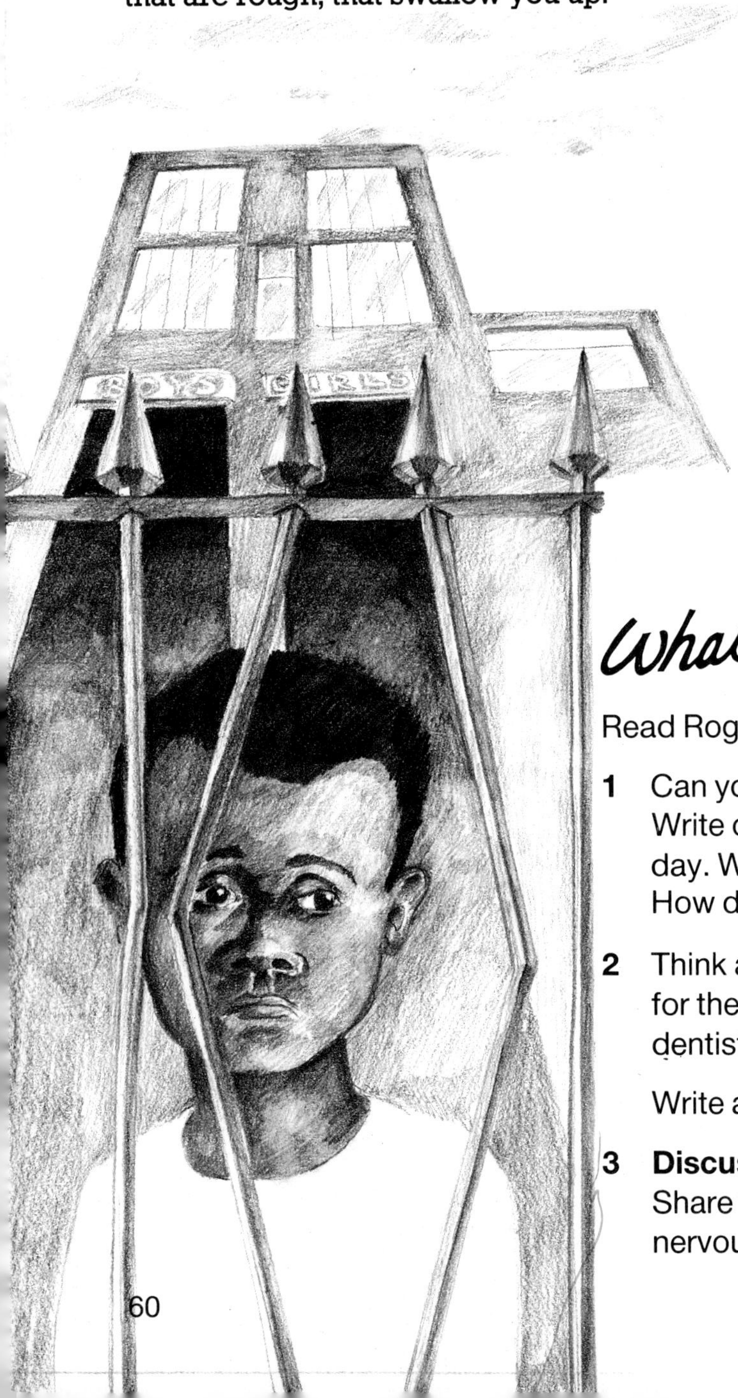

What you do

Read Roger McGough's poem about the first day at school.

1 Can you remember your first day at school? Write out what you remember about that first day. Was it what you expected – better or worse? How did things turn out?

2 Think about other times in your life when you did something for the first time: joined the Cubs or Brownies; went to the dentist; went on holiday without your Mum to a relative.

Write about the way it was. Call your writing 'For the first time'.

3 **Discussion time**
Share your experiences with your friends. If you were a little nervous that was natural. Things generally turn out all right.

Things to come

Do you feel nervous about another first day – going to the secondary school?
Do you imagine huge children ready to bully and tease?
Great buildings to get lost in?
New teachers and subjects you won't understand?

It won't really be like that. There will be plenty of friends and people to help you.

Very soon you will be as used to it as you are to your junior school.

Let's think about what it will really be like.

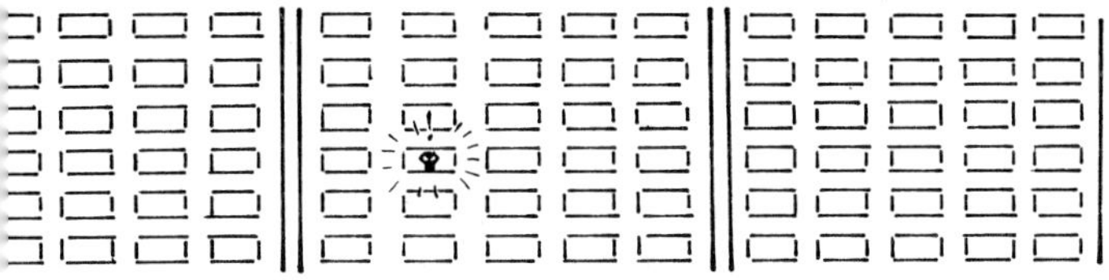

What you do

1 Read these suggestions and, when you have thought about them, write about your hopes for your new school:
   What do you look forward to most?
   What, if anything, worries you about your new school?
   What do you think will be most different from your junior school?
   Do you know any children from the secondary school? What do they say about it? They may try to tell you all sorts of stories just to scare you.

2 **Discussion time**
Share your speculations about going to the secondary school with your friends. Did they have the same thoughts as you? Can you think of ways of making your move to the new school easier? You probably make visits before you go.

3 When you have all finished your writing your teacher may like to send your ideas on to the secondary school. The teachers there would find them very helpful in making you welcome next term.

Diaries

Do you keep a diary? In diaries people not only put down what has happened during that day but also their thoughts. They reflect on what has happened and how they feel.

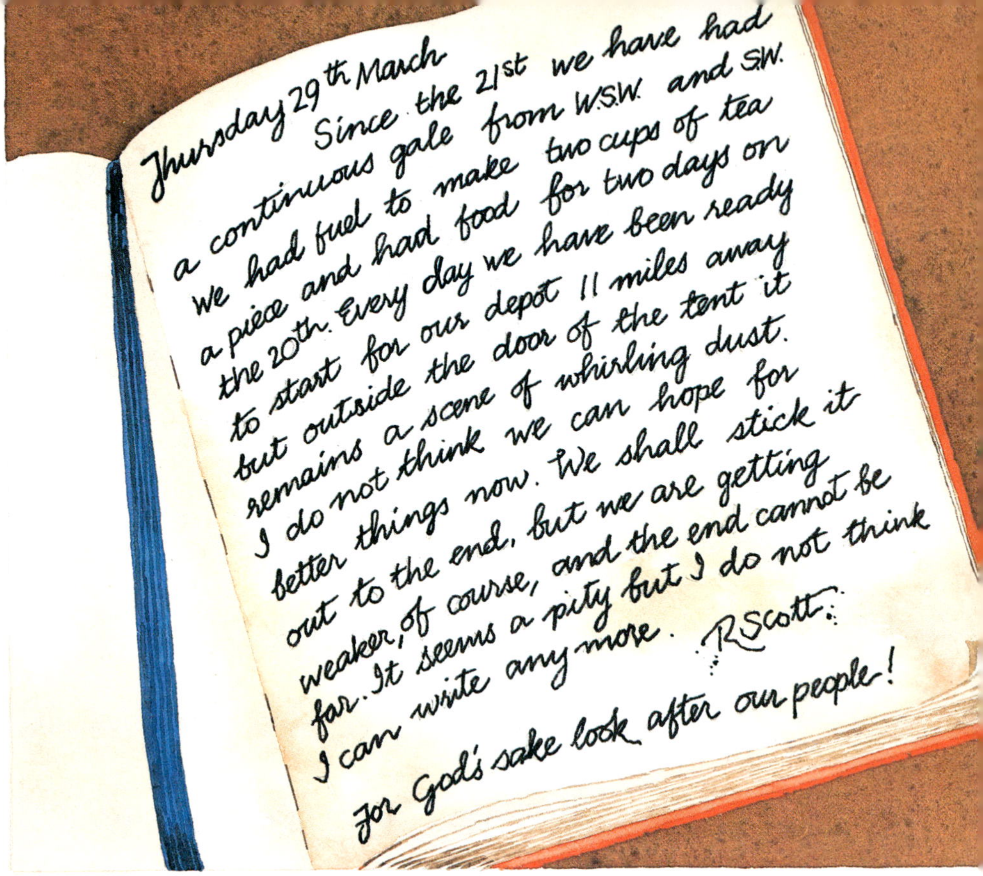

Captain Scott's diary of his expedition to the South Pole is one of the most famous diaries. There are many others that are well known – by people like Anne Frank, Edith Holden and Samuel Pepys.

Why not keep a special diary for your last term at junior school? It could be very interesting to read when you are grown up.

What you do

This will be a special diary, not just a news book. Make a suitable book, or use a school exercise book. Decorate the cover and give it a title like 'The diary of Jim Smith' or 'The diary of a 20th-century schoolgirl'. It will be better with a stiff cover.

During the week make notes of interesting things that happened: a visit you made, a good game you played, anything unusual you saw, as well as ordinary things. On Friday write the diary.

Our private diaries are just for us. We can write as little or as much as we want. We can write down how we feel and know no-one will be angry or laugh at us. We can ask questions of ourselves. We can help ourselves cope with things that annoy us by writing them down.

Your teacher will help you get going if you need ideas.

	1st Term				2nd Term				3rd Term			
Types of writing	*1st Qtr*	*2nd Qtr*	*3rd Qtr*	*4th Qtr*	*1st Qtr*	*2nd Qtr*	*3rd Qtr*	*4th Qtr*	*1st Qtr*	*2nd Qtr*	*3rd Qtr*	*4th Qtr*
Opinions												
Descriptions												
Express feelings												
Instructions												
Plans												
Stories												
Conversations												
Predictions												
Directions												
Present arguments												
Poetry												
To persuade												
To report												
To record												
To justify												
To reflect												

Social studies	SS	Language session	LS		
Environmental studies	ES	Religious education	RE	Nature study	NS
Science	SC	Integrated project	IP	Mathematics	M

Note to the teacher

This series aims to broaden the range of writing encountered by older junior and middle school children and to draw them into areas of written work that have been stressed by recent major reports but are nevertheless often neglected in school.

Each book contains eight units. A unit contains work for several lessons and thus, overall, each book should provide a range of written work stretching over a full school year. The units may be used in any order as the teacher sees a need for experience in a particular type of writing.

The written work is intended to be challenging but is based on topics which draw upon experience common to most children. There is therefore no need for elaborate preparation by the teacher or preliminary activity by the children before they begin to write. There is, however, an emphasis on discussion as a class before any writing is undertaken, and in the sharing of the responses in groups afterwards. In many of the activities there is the opportunity for children to work together in pairs or in small groups.

The response asked of the children will lead them into new kinds of writing and make fresh demands upon their imagination and creativity. It is therefore suggested that in most units teachers concentrate on the content of the pupil's response rather than the technical accuracy with which it is expressed.

All Kinds of Writing may be used in classes of mixed ability. The written activity allows for responses at the level appropriate to each individual child.

The chart printed on p63 is intended to help the teacher plot the types of writing the class has covered as the term progresses. A teacher making such a chart for his or her own use (it is not intended that there should be a copy for each child)

a will ensure that the class is encountering a range of writing modes and be able to spot the gaps;

b have some indication of the source of the various types of writing undertaken, across the curriculum.

Thus ES in the Description row would mean that Environmental studies had provided an opportunity for some descriptive writing. RE in the Story row would mean that a story had been written in Religious education.

Teachers will thus be alerted not only to neglect of any one type of writing but also as to whether they are making full use of the whole curriculum as a source for variety in written work. Poems can flow as readily from a nature lesson as from a language lesson. Again, the importance of discussion between teacher and children before activities are undertaken is underlined.

R. W. Forward
1986

The author would like to thank Miss Isobel Gaffney, Headteacher of Rosary R.C. Junior School, Hampstead, for her most helpful suggestions. He would also like to thank Mr John Gulliver, Primary Adviser for English, Devon, who first introduced him to the full list of writing areas used in this book.

Published by the Press Syndicate of the University of Cambridge
The Pitt Building, Trumpington Street, Cambridge CB2 1RP
32 East 57th Street, New York, NY 10022, USA
10 Stamford Road, Oakleigh, Melbourne 3166, Australia

First published 1987

Printed in Great Britain by Scotprint Ltd, Musselburgh, Scotland

ISBN 0 521 33986 3

Designed by Ann Samuel

Illustrated by Terry Burton, Hemesh Alles, Sheila Faichney, Di Lorriman, Mike Dodd, Barry Rowe

Typeset by Goodfellow & Egan, Cambridge

Acknowledgements

The author and publisher would like to thank the following for permission to reproduce material in this book:

p.16 'The Canary' by Ogden Nash, from *I wouldn't have missed it*, Andre Deutsch Ltd; p.16 'Reflection on babies' © 1940 by Ogden Nash from *Verses from 1929 on*, reproduced by permission of Curtis Brown Ltd, London, and Little, Brown and Company; p.16 'My Teacher' by Kevin Brown; p.17 'Bertha Brown' by Andrew Ridley; p.19 'On the Ning Nang Nong' by Spike Milligan; p.20 'My Mother saw a dancing bear' by Charles Causley, from *Figgie Hobbin*, Macmillan; p.21 'Take one home for the kiddies' by Philip Larkin, from *The Whitsun Weddings*, reprinted by permission of Faber and Faber Ltd; p.22 'Vulture' by X. J. Kennedy, from *Allsorts 7*, ed. Anne Thwaite, Methuen Children's Books; p.22 Mrs McHingy' by Diana Harland; p.54 'Grass' by Aileen Fisher; p.55 'When I was your age' by Michael Frayn, from *Allsorts Book 7*, ed. Anne Thwaite,Methuen Children's Books; p.60 'First Day at School' by Roger McGough, from *In the Classroom*, Jonathan Cape Ltd.

Every effort has been made to reach copyright holders; the publishers would be glad to hear from anyone whose rights they have unwittingly infringed.

In the same series
All Kinds of Writing Book 1